I HAD TO CHOOSE

A Man Reflects on His Sexuality and the Choices He Made

DAVID A. ROBINSON

LifeRich PUBLISHING

This book is a work of non-fiction. Unless otherwise noted, the author and the publisher make no explicit guarantees as to the accuracy of the information contained in this book.

LifeRich Publishing is a registered trademark of The Reader's Digest Association, Inc.

LifeRich Publishing books may be ordered through booksellers or by contacting:

LifeRich Publishing
1663 Liberty Drive
Bloomington, IN 47403
www.liferichpublishing.com
1 (888) 238-8637

Because of the dynamic nature of the Internet, any web addresses or links contained in this book may have changed since publication and may no longer be valid. The views expressed in this work are solely those of the author and do not necessarily reflect the views of the publisher, and the publisher hereby disclaims any responsibility for them.

Any people depicted in stock imagery provided by Getty Images are models, and such images are being used for illustrative purposes only. Certain stock imagery © Getty Images.

Scripture taken from the New King James Version®. Copyright © 1982 by Thomas Nelson. Used by permission. All rights reserved.

ISBN: 978-1-4897-2739-8 (sc)
ISBN: 978-1-4897-2740-4 (e)

Library of Congress Control Number: 2020901429

Print information available on the last page.

LifeRich Publishing rev. date: 02/25/2020

CONTENTS

INTRODUCTION

This book is for people who have homosexual urges but wish to fall in love with someone of the opposite sex. I tell how I did it. It wasn't always easy, but it was my choice.

Some people say we have no choice about our sexuality. If a fifteen-year-old boy is sexually excited looking at muscular, athletic boys, some people tell him, "You're gay. You have no choice about it. Date boys, not girls. Be who you are. You can't change who you are."

It wasn't always this way. In 1968 I was that fifteen-year-old boy. I was sexually excited looking at muscular, athletic boys. It happened to me repeatedly from early 1967 to

1

early 1969. Back then, almost no one told me to date boys. Homosexuality was taboo in the 1960s. Almost everyone told me to date girls. In 2020 there are more openly gay people than in 1968. In 2020 if a fifteen-year-old boy is sexually excited looking at muscular, athletic boys, many gay people and some straight people will tell him to date boys. They'll tell him he has "no choice."

But the boy must eventually make a choice. Months or years from now, he may want romance and will have to choose a companion—male or female. Which will he choose? Or is his only choice male? He may want to marry. He must choose whether to marry a man or woman. Or is his only choice a man?

Despite my homosexual urges, I chose to date females. I eventually married a woman and am very happy with her. We've been a couple since 1997, married since 2003. I am sixty-seven in 2020.

My sexual journey had nothing to do with religion. Some people—Christian, Jewish, Muslim, other faith, or no faith—have homosexual urges but want, or wish, to marry someone of the opposite sex. This book is for them. Whether their motivation is religious or secular, this book is for them. It tells how I did it. Should you do what I did? I don't know. I have no opinion on whether you should do it. You must decide for yourself.

If you have no desire to marry someone of the opposite sex, this book is not for you. You are welcome to read it, but I'm not telling you what to desire. Decide for yourself what you desire. This book is for people who have homosexual urges but desire to happily marry someone of the opposite sex. I tell how I dealt with those urges.

This book isn't "therapy" or "conversion therapy." I am not a therapist, so this book isn't therapy. It is not a clinical guide. I am not a psychologist, medical doctor, or clergyman. I'm an ordinary man telling my own true story. Are you like me? Is your sexual orientation like mine? I don't know. Decide for yourself. The word *therapy* implies there is something wrong with someone. It implies curing someone. I am not saying anyone is wrong. I am not trying to cure or convert anyone. Perhaps it's a matter of semantics, but in my opinion a man who has homosexual urges and wishes to fall in love with a woman is not trying to "convert." He has a penis. She has a vagina. He is anatomically designed to have sex with her. He is trying to do what he is designed, and wishes, to do.

How shall we label people who have homosexual urges but wish to marry someone of the opposite sex? Gay? Straight? Homosexual? Heterosexual? Bisexual? Queer? Questioning? Pansexual? Let us not label these people. Those labels are often misleading and unfair. They mean different things to different people. To many people, "gay" means homosexual urges—regardless of whether a person gives in to those urges. I've heard people say about a man (let's call him John), "John is gay but is married to a woman" (let's call her Mary). What does that mean? Does it mean John has sex with Mary but also has sex with a man on the side? Does it mean John has sex with a man and does not have sex with Mary? Does it mean John had sex with a man before John married Mary but now has sex only with Mary? Does it mean John fantasizes about a man when John has sex with Mary? Does it mean Mary has some features that these people regard as manly? We don't know what these people mean. And even if we know, sometimes they are mistaken. Sometimes they don't know what John does or thinks. Sometimes they are just speculating.

Some people label John bisexual. What does that mean? If John had sex with a man in 1980 but has had sex with only Mary since 1990, is John bisexual? What does it mean to "have sex?" If a fifteen-year-old boy gets an erection when he looks at muscular, athletic boys in the gym shower but never actually touches them, or touches them on the arm or butt, or fantasizes about them, will people say he is gay? Is he "having sex?" What if, when he turns sixteen or seventeen, he dates only girls? What if he eventually marries a woman? Is he gay? Was he gay? Is he ex-gay? Is he bisexual?

Those labels are almost meaningless. I try to avoid them as much as possible. I try to avoid the term "sexual orientation." "Orientation" can mean several different things. It can mean one's thinking or outlook. It can mean the direction someone is facing or tends to go. It is not necessarily a constraint. It does not necessarily dictate what we will do. Did my sexual orientation dictate my choice? My sexual orientation influenced, but did not dictate, my choice. It limited my choice of females, but not to zero. All men limit their choice of females. No man finds all women attractive. Most men find some women attractive. I found some (not many, but some) women attractive.

Some people say I'm a product of my time. I was sixteen in 1969, when homosexuality was taboo. Homosexual behavior was a crime in many states in 1969. Some people say my only choice in 1969 was to date girls. Some people say homosexuality is more accepted today than in 1969. If I were sixteen today, some people would say my only choice is to date boys.

What would I choose if I were sixteen today? I can't know for certain. I am sixty-seven today. I wish I could be sixteen today but I can't. I can only surmise what I'd choose if I were sixteen today. I surmise I would want the option—maybe not the *requirement*, but the *option*—to date girls. I would not want to be told, "You're gay. You have no choice about it. Your only choice is to date boys."

Why would I want the option to date girls? Why would a boy with homosexual urges in 2020 even think about dating a girl? If, as many people claim, homosexuality is more accepted today than it was in 1969, why would—or might—he want to date a girl? I can think of five reasons. Whether they are good reasons is debatable. Some LGBTQ people will say these are not good reasons. Good or not, these are reasons a sixteen-year-old boy with homosexual urges in 2020 may want the option to date girls and eventually marry a woman.

First, although same-sex marriage has been legal throughout the United States since 2015, my guess is that approximately 95 percent of weddings taking place in the United States in 2020 are male-female weddings, not same-sex weddings. I was unable to find any official national statistics on this. My guess is based on statistics I found from Hawaii, New Hampshire, and Virginia. Same-sex marriage has been legal in Hawaii since 2013. According to the Hawaii Department of Health Vital Statistics,[1] 4.8 percent (1,044 of 21,646) of weddings that took place in Hawaii in 2018 were same-sex

---

[1] https://health.hawaii.gov/vitalstatistics/preliminary-marriage-total-same-sex/ (last visited Feb. 21, 2020).

weddings. That was down a little from 6.2 percent (1,375 of 22,228) in 2016 and 5.2 percent (1,147 of 21,908) in 2017. Same-sex marriage has been legal in New Hampshire since 2010. Approximately 3 percent of weddings that took place in New Hampshire in 2018 were same-sex weddings, down from 6.2 percent in 2013.[2] Same-sex marriage has been legal in Virginia since 2014. Approximately 4 percent of Virginia weddings since 2014 have been same-sex weddings.[3] I am guessing that in most of the United States the figure is between 4 and 5 percent, but let's round it up to 5 percent. The boy may want to "go with the crowd"—marry a woman—rather than join the 5 percent minority.

Second, the boy may look at the male and female sex organs and conclude that the male sex organ is designed to fit into the female sex organ. That is not the only place it can fit, and that is not all it is designed to do. But he may believe

---

[2] David Brooks, "Same-sex marriages have declined in N.H. and neighboring states," *Concord Monitor*, Feb. 9, 2019, https://www.concordmonitor.com/gay-marriage-nh-weddings-22641430 (last visited Feb. 21, 2020).

[3] Virginia Capital News Service, "4% of Marriages in Virginia Have Been Same-Sex Unions," https://patch.com/virginia/across-va/4-marriages-virginia-have-been-same-sex-unions (last visited Feb. 21, 2020).

that the male sex organ is designed to fit into the female sex organ. He may want to live accordingly. He may believe that only a man and woman, not two men, can "become one."

Third, he may want to reproduce. He may want to reproduce the "natural" way—by heterosexual intercourse—not by adopting a child or conceiving a child with a surrogate. He may want to marry the woman with whom he conceives a child. A child is dependent on his or her parents for the first twenty or so years of life. He may believe that the man and woman who create the child should stay together and raise the child together.

Fourth, he may believe that homosexuality is contrary to the teaching of his religion.

Fifth, he may worry that some people will scorn and discriminate against him if he dates boys and marries a man.

There is a sixth possible reason he may want to be heterosexual. I will not discuss it much, because I am not qualified to discuss it much. I will not ignore it, either. The sixth reason is health. Some people believe, correctly or incorrectly, that men who have sex with men are more likely to contract HIV than men who have sex with women. Whether there is a correlation, causation, or other relationship, I am not qualified to say. It suffices to say that health reasons, founded or unfounded, cause some men with homosexual urges to want to be heterosexual.

I am not urging the boy to be, or try to be, heterosexual. It is up to the boy. He should decide what he wants to do: date a boy, date a girl, marry a man, marry a woman, go to college, not go to college. These are decisions he has to make for himself. I'm not telling him what to do. I am simply explaining why some boys with homosexual urges may want the option of dating girls. They may have more options than some people are telling them.

CHAPTER 1

I Am What I Am,
but What Am I?

I was born in 1953. Like most boys, I played only with boys until I was around twelve. If a boy had a girlfriend, other boys snickered. Many boys thought girls were kind of "yucky."

This changed around the time I turned twelve. Most of my classmates were turning, or close to turning, thirteen. Parties and get-togethers became coed. There were school dances. Boys danced with girls. Boys kissed girls. Boys and girls started thinking about dating. Most boys wanted to date girls. I thought I wanted to date girls.

But my body signaled that I want to date boys. As a freshman at Longmeadow (Massachusetts) High School in the spring of 1967, I began having erections. I had them when I looked at boys. Not all boys, but some boys. In particular, muscular boys. On several occasions during my freshman, sophomore, and junior years, I had an erection while naked in the gym locker room looking at one muscular boy or another. One time someone—I don't recall if he was a student or teacher—saw it. He told me that the penis, when erect, is designed to fit into a vagina. It was his way of telling me that sex should be between a male and female, not two males. I thought about it. It made sense to me. It is anatomically correct. It is how babies are made. I concluded that dating, romance, sex, and marriage should be between a male and female.

When I was fifteen in the summer of 1968, I was in a swimming pool with a male friend, also fifteen. I was sexually attracted to him. I kissed his arm. I thought about boys when I masturbated in 1967–68. I apologize, a little, for talking about masturbation. It is an awkward topic. But this book is about sex. Masturbation is part of the sex lives of many teenagers and adults. Some religions frown on masturbation. The Catholic Church frowns on it but is more lenient about it with teens and some adults, depending on psychological and social factors.[4]

Later in this book I will describe in detail my sex life from ages fifteen to forty-four. At forty-four I met the woman who would become my wife. I will state now, however, that I have never touched a man's penis except my own. I have never kissed a man on the mouth, and except for kissing my male friend's arm in 1968, never had any type of physical sexual contact with a male. Therefore, some readers of this book may argue I am not gay and never was. But they are looking at me now, age sixty-seven. If a fifteen-year-old boy today gets an erection looking at muscular boys in the gym shower, many people will label him gay, especially if it happens repeatedly over a two-year period as it did to me. Many people, especially LGBTQ people, will tell him to date boys, not girls. "Be who you are," they'll tell him. It reminds me of the song "I Am

---

[4] *Catechism of the Catholic Church* ¶ 2352, https://www.vatican.va/archive/ENG0015/__P85.HTM (last visited Feb. 21, 2020).

What I Am" from the gay-themed Broadway musical *La Cage aux Folles.*

I am what I am, but what am I? I am male. That's what I am. I have a male sex organ. From what I see in my biology textbook, the male sex organ, when erect, is designed to fit into the female sex organ. Should I live by that design, or should I live homosexually? That is the question. It was the question in 1968. From the beginning of time, people with homosexual urges have asked themselves that question.

Be who you are? I decided to be who I want to be, not who some people say I am. Some people reading this book will say I was gay at fifteen and am gay at sixty-seven. It is semantics. It depends on how one defines the word *gay*. Regardless of how one defines it, I have lived the sexual life I wanted—chose—to live. Since age sixteen, I have had sex with women only. That was my choice. I'm not saying it was the right choice. I'm saying it was my choice. It was a choice not entirely consistent with my "orientation."

From ages sixteen to forty-four, I had a strong sex drive, but there were very few women I wanted to have sex with. If

I saw a hundred women my age, there were maybe five that I wanted to be intimate with. That is, there were five who I thought I might want to be intimate with if I got to know them better. Most, if not all, of the five were muscular, or muscular relative to other women: muscular legs, muscular arms, muscular abdominals, or muscular glutes. Did you ever notice the similarity between the words "muscular" and "masculine"? I didn't until I began writing this. It jolted me. I had an epiphany, of sorts. Something occurred to me that never occurred to me before. Most women that I have found sexually attractive have been muscular. Does this mean I am a latent homosexual? Does it mean I'd really prefer to be with a man but to cover up that preference—or perhaps for moral, religious, or "public image" reasons—settle for the "next best thing": a muscular woman? If you define me by what I do, I am straight. I have had sex only with women. If you define me by what I think about, I'm not sure what I am.

Here is my additional response to people who say I am not and never was gay. Many LGBTQ people and their allies are trying to pass legislation that bans efforts to change the sexual orientation of a person younger than age eighteen.

They call such efforts "conversion therapy," and they want to ban it. They want to make it illegal for a psychologist or other licensed health counselor to tell a boy like me—fifteen and attracted to boys—that the male sex organ is designed to fit into the female sex organ. They want a boy like me to regard the female sex organ as one of numerous places the male sex organ can fit. They want a boy like me to be gay and stay gay. They oppose efforts to change him, even if he wants to change. So if they argue that my sexual orientation at fifteen in 1968 was not gay, why do they label a similar fifteen-year-old boy today gay? Why do they try to prevent efforts to change him even if he *wants* to change? In chapter 6, I discuss "conversion therapy" and the movement to ban it.

That conversation in the Longmeadow High School gym locker room in 1968, when I was told an erect penis should interact with a female, not another male, was "conversion therapy." You might not think of it as such, but it was. It was an effort to change my sexual orientation. Today such a conversation would be illegal in some states and cities in the United States, depending on the job title of the adult who is telling the child. In those states and cities, it is illegal for a psychologist or other licensed health counselor to say or do anything that might change the child's sexual orientation, even if the child wants to change. If the counselor knows that the boy has homosexual urges, it is illegal for the counselor to help the boy be heterosexual. Telling the boy that the penis is designed to fit into the vagina tells the boy that heterosexual sex is normal and natural and that homosexual sex is not. It might cause the boy to be, or try to be, heterosexual. The state government might revoke the counselor's license.

At age forty-four I fell in love with a woman. We've been a couple ever since. In the next three chapters, I'll take you on the long and winding road—ages sixteen to forty-four—that led me to her door, to borrow from a Beatles song.

CHAPTER 2

The Long and Winding Road

I associate the Beatles song "The Long and Winding Road" with an important milepost in my life. It was the number-one song on the Billboard Hot 100 the day I graduated from high school in June 1970. It marks the end of my childhood and beginning of my adulthood. "The Long and Winding Road" is a fitting description of the sexual journey I began in 1967 and would travel for the next thirty years until I met my wife in 1997.

That locker room conversation in which I was instructed that an erect penis is designed to fit into a vagina occurred shortly before I turned sixteen. As a result of that conversation, I made a decision when I turned sixteen in early 1969: if I have a romance with someone, it will be with a female, not a male. Why? Was it peer pressure? Parental pressure? Societal pressure? Religious pressure? Was it because homosexuality was unpopular then? It was none of those things. It was what I just said: The penis, when erect, is designed to fit into the vagina. I decided to do what I am anatomically designed to do.

Looking back at that decision now, fifty-one years later, many LGBTQ people would say it was the wrong decision. They'd say I would have enjoyed sex with males. They'd say I should have married a man after same-sex marriage became legal. I view the decision I made in 1969 the way I view the decision I made in 2003, when I decided to marry the woman I met in 1997. Both the 1969 and 2003 decisions limited my sexual options. My 1969 decision limited me to females only. My 2003 decision limited me to one female only. Some people prefer to have more options. That's up to them. I am satisfied with the decisions I made.

I don't remember hearing about homosexuality when I was in elementary school, middle school, or high school. I don't remember hearing anything negative or positive about it. In elementary school, if a boy was unathletic or effeminate, the bullies might call him a "fairy," but I did not know exactly what "fairy" meant. I'm not sure they knew. I might have heard the word "f-gg-t." I thought it was synonymous with "fairy." I heard the word *gay*, but in the 1960s, gay meant happy. Not until 1970, when I graduated from high school and entered college, did gay mean homosexual.

In early 1969 I saw the movie *Oliver!* It won the Academy Award for Best Picture of 1968. There was a beautiful, buxom actress, Shani Wallis, who played Nancy. I was sexually aroused watching her. That is the first time I can remember being sexually aroused looking at or thinking about a woman. Thereafter, I developed a keen interest in a TV show I had never been interested in before: "I Dream of Jeannie." Watching Barbara Eden in her genie outfit sexually aroused me. She was buxom and had excellent abdominal muscles. Other TV and movie actresses I was attracted to in 1969 or the early '70s were Raquel Welch, Ann-Margret, Mitzi

Gaynor, Sophia Loren, and Pam Grier. They were buxom and had excellent abdominal muscles. I felt heterosexual. But which did I like more: bosom or muscle? The older I got, the clearer the answer became: muscle.

My first date was on the last Saturday night of the 1960s: December 27, 1969. I had two dates with her. I had one or two dates with other girls in early 1970.

In April 1970, near the end of my high school senior year, I went by myself on a bus trip to visit George Washington University, a college I was considering. The ride to Washington DC was four hundred miles. I wanted something to read on the bus. At a bus stop, I bought the May 1970 issue of *Playboy* magazine. The centerfold had really good abdominal muscles and big breasts.

In 1970 a book was published that became for many people "the bible" on sex. I don't mean the Holy Bible. I mean the book *Everything You Always Wanted to Know About Sex* (*But Were Afraid to Ask)*, by Dr. David Reuben, a psychiatrist. Reuben's book became enormously popular. It seemed like everyone was reading it and talking about it. I read it. Four decades later, when I began writing this, I decided to revisit Reuben's book. First I had to find a copy. I didn't see it in the bookstores (physical bookstores) I went to or in public libraries near me. This surprised me because it was a classic. It sold millions of copies. Why couldn't I find one now?

I purchased one on Amazon's website. After reading what it said about homosexuality, I know why it is hard to find today. It has become politically incorrect. It is probably the only book that almost everyone over the age of sixty today has heard of but almost no one under the age of forty today has. Try finding it in a library or physical bookstore today. You may have difficulty. (Don't confuse the book with the 1972 Woody Allen movie of the same title. I've never seen the movie.)

Reuben's book has a question and answer format. On page 162 (Bantam ed. 1971):

Q. Couldn't homosexuals just be born that way?

A. A lot of homosexuals would like to think so. They prefer you to consider their problem the equivalent of a club foot or birthmark; just something to struggle through life with.

Reuben then added, "This explanation is a little tragic. It implies that all homosexuals are condemned without appeal to a life some of them say they enjoy so much. Actually, for those who want to change, there is a chance."

He continued:

Q. How?

A. If a homosexual who wants to renounce homosexuality finds a psychiatrist who knows how to cure homosexuality, he has every chance of becoming a happy, well-adjusted heterosexual.

That is what Reuben said in 1970. It did not sit well with the gay community, where many vehemently opposed his assertion that homosexuality can be "changed" or "cured." Many helped persuade some mental-health associations to oppose Reuben's assertion and declare that homosexuality is not a mental illness. Many tried to discourage psychiatrists and psychologists from offering therapies relating to a person's sexual orientation. If a man steals, overeats, smokes cigarettes, commits adultery, fears heights, or has some other issue going on in his head, mental-health professionals are encouraged to help him. If a man is attracted to men but wants to marry a woman, many people in the gay community discourage mental-health professionals from trying to help him marry a woman. Recently they persuaded eighteen states—California, Colorado, Connecticut, Delaware, Hawaii, Illinois, Maine, Maryland, Nevada, New Hampshire, New Jersey, New Mexico, New York, Oregon, Rhode Island, Utah, Vermont, Washington, and the District of Columbia—to pass laws that prohibit mental-health professionals from trying to help a child (younger than eighteen) who has homosexual urges be heterosexual. These laws ban what these laws call "conversion therapy" (or "sexual orientation change efforts") on minors. A nineteenth state, Massachusetts, prohibits health care providers from any practice "that attempts or purports to impose change of" a child's sexual orientation or gender identity (Mass. General Laws chapter 112, section 275). The word *impose* is notable. Is Massachusetts prohibiting forced (imposed) conversion therapy but allowing conversion therapy a child requests? I don't know. It will be interesting to see. I devote chapter 6 to the subject of conversion therapy and the effort to ban it. (*Important*: To learn the law pertaining to conversion therapy in your state, read the law yourself or ask a lawyer. Don't just read what my book says about it. These laws are worded somewhat differently from state to state.)

I went to my senior prom with a girl from my class. It was our only date. I graduated from high school in June 1970.

My first romance—more than two dates with the same girl—was a summer romance in 1970. Looking back at it today, it portended the many problems I would have with women. We were both seventeen. We worked at a local McDonald's that summer. She had a very good figure and a cute face. She looked great in the McDonald's uniform women employees wore. She and I played tennis and went swimming. In her tennis outfit and two-piece swimsuit, which were more revealing that her McDonald's uniform, I was not as impressed as I thought I would be. This is not a reflection on her but on me. I had a problem. I was not quite as excited about a female body as I thought I would be. I was hoping her body would look like the body I saw in the May 1970 *Playboy* centerfold. Her body was good but not quite that good. Was that my only problem? Was my "orientation," which perhaps was not 100 percent heterosexual, also a problem, or is it part of the same problem? I don't know. Your guess is as good as mine on that. This would happen to me many times over the next twenty-seven years. I ended the relationship when the summer ended.

As you'll see in the next few chapters, it took me a long time to find a lasting relationship with a woman. That is something I have in common with many people who identify as gay: great difficulty establishing a lasting intimate relationship with someone of the opposite sex. Some people who identify as gay never try to. Many try at one time or another. Will they try again? Should they? That is up to them. If they find this book helpful in making that decision, the book serves its purpose.

As I stated earlier, religion had nothing to do with my sexual journey. Some people with homosexual urges behave heterosexually for religious reasons. I am not one of them. If I were an atheist, which I am not, I would have the same views on homosexuality as I have now.

If I were an atheist, I would say this: Men, not "god" (small g), wrote the bible (small b). Those men thought homosexual sex is wrong and contrary to anatomical design. Those men thought the male sex organ is designed to be inserted into the female sex organ. That is how people reproduce. Men wrote the bible to tell people what they (the men who wrote the bible) believe is the right way to live. Homosexual sex is wrong not because the bible says it's wrong but the other way around: The bible says homosexual sex is wrong because the men who wrote the bible thought homosexual sex is wrong. The bible merely reflects the thinking of the men who wrote it.

To express moral views while separating church and state, some people use the word *nature* rather than "god." An Oklahoma court had to decide whether the crime of "sodomy" includes oral sex or only anal sex. The court held:

> In the order of nature the nourishment of the human body is accomplished by the operation of the alimentary canal, beginning with the mouth and ending with the rectum. In this process food enters the first opening, the mouth,

and residuum and waste are discharged through the nether opening of the rectum. The natural functions of the organs for the reproduction of the species are entirely different from those of the nutritive system. It is self-evident that the use of either opening of the alimentary canal for the purpose of sexual copulation is against the natural design of the human body. In other words, it is an offense against nature. There can be no difference in reason whether such an unnatural coition takes place in the mouth or in the fundament—at one end of the alimentary canal or the other. The moral filthiness and iniquity against which the statute [prohibiting sodomy] is aimed is the same in both cases.[5]

Do most people today agree with what the Oklahoma court said? I don't know. I think many people agree with it today. Almost everyone agrees with the first few sentences. Some people disagree with the last few sentences.

---

[5] *Ex parte De Ford*, 14 Okla. Crim. App. 133, 168 P. 58 (1917).

In August 1970, women (and many men) celebrated the fiftieth anniversary of the ratification of the Nineteenth Amendment to the U.S. Constitution. The Nineteenth Amendment gave women the right to vote. A new term entered popular culture in the summer of 1970: women's lib, or women's liberation, or the women's liberation movement.

In the next chapter, I will tell you about my college and law school years. In September 1970 I left my parents' home in Massachusetts and moved into a large dormitory in Washington DC, three blocks from the White House.

CHAPTER 3

Mr. Robinson Goes
to Washington

In September 1970 I enrolled as a freshman at George Washington University (GWU). My problems with women continued. If I looked at a hundred female classmates, I found perhaps five sexually attractive. I had difficulty landing a date with any of the five. Either I was too shy to ask, or I asked and was rejected. I don't think I had any dates my freshman year.

A few months into my first semester, I was introduced to an upperclassman. Rumor had it (in 1970) he is gay, but I didn't think about it much. I was flattered that an upperclassman showed an interest in me. He had a posh apartment. He invited me there one night. I accepted his invitation. We talked about women and dating. I told him I find few women sexually attractive. When I find one, I am either too bashful to ask her for a date or I ask and she refuses.

He replied, "You have ruled out every woman in the world." He was essentially telling me: You're gay. He did not make a pass at me, as far as I could tell, but he asked if knew about "gay lib" (a variation of the new term "women's lib").

A classmate of mine knew I went to this upperclassman's apartment. A week or so later, the classmate said to me, "Dave, you haven't been quite the same since you went to his apartment." Many years later, I learned that this classmate is gay. He never made a pass at me. I think he was just curious as to what happened in that apartment. Did something happen that caused me to be, or feel, gay?

Sometime during my freshman year, a new movie was shown on campus: *The Boys in the Band*. It taught me that I have an option besides women. That movie affected me profoundly. I saw it only that one time, so my recollection of it might not be 100 percent accurate. With the help of some information I found on the Internet, here is what happened in the movie. A man named Alan is attracted to men but marries a woman. Unable to completely disregard his homosexual urges, he and some other men who question their own sexuality attend a gay party. At the end of the party, the host encourages Alan to call (on the phone) a man Alan loves and tell the man that Alan loves him. Alan thinks about it, then makes the call. He tells the person who answers, "I love you." Who did he call? His wife.

I don't know if *The Boys in the Band* is shown much these days. The ending has, from what I have read online, become controversial. It is a different ending than many people in the gay community want to see today. Alan chose his wife over a man. I have thought about that ending many times. Regardless of what sexual thoughts go through a man's mind, at some point he has to make a decision: With whom will he share his penis? A woman or a man? Alan chose a woman. So did I.

A revival of the stage version of *The Boys in the Band* is running in Chicago in early 2020. A film version is planned for later in 2020. I don't know if the story and script differ from the 1970 version.

My sex life in 1971 and '72 is best described by a popular song of that time: "Just My Imagination." In the song, a man talks about the woman he loves. Then he admits, "But in reality, she doesn't even know me. It's just my imagination." My sex life consisted of fantasizing. I won't tell you the details. I had a few—very few—dates in 1971 and '72.

My first serious romance was at GWU in 1973. When I got to know this woman a little in late 1972, I liked her personality but was not attracted to her looks. She looked okay but was not among the women I really had my eye on. She was not buxom. She usually wore jeans. I liked her as a friend but did not want to date her.

One day I was facing a stairway. Only the lower stairs were visible to me. I saw a pair of legs descending, and in the first instant I saw them, I could not see who they were attached to. They were gorgeous—slender ankles leading to voluptuous, shapely (muscular) calves, beautiful thighs, and her short skirt.

As she continued down the stairs, I saw her face. It was her—the one I liked personally but whose looks I thought were just okay. Suddenly I was in love. She also had good forearms, triceps, and abdominal muscles. When I suddenly showed a romantic interest in her in the spring of 1973, she rejected me. She repeatedly told me she does not want to date me.

I was a mess that summer while at home in Massachusetts. I thought about her all the time. I visited her at her home in upstate New York in June. It was a nice visit, but she still resisted me romantically. When we both returned to GWU in September and she continued to reject me, I fell into a deep, serious depression. Then, in early October, she decided to give me a chance. We became boyfriend and girlfriend. I was thrilled, or thought I was thrilled, for the next three months.

Suddenly, on New Year's Eve (or New Year's Day), the thrill was gone. I don't remember everything that went through my head during those twenty-four or so hours, but here is what I remember: I was home for Christmas vacation. My girlfriend was at her parents' home in upstate New York, three hundred miles away. I decided I want to be with her on New Year's Eve. I call her that morning (Dec. 31, 1973) and ask if I can come to her home that night. She says yes. Due to the Arab oil embargo following the Yom Kippur War in October 1973, gasoline is in short supply, so I can't take my parents' car. I go to the Springfield bus station and board a bus for upstate New York.

At a bus stop in Albany, I buy a magazine. You guessed it: *Playboy*. I did as I did on my bus trip to Washington in 1970. This new issue—January 1974—was no ordinary issue. It was *Playboy*'s twentieth anniversary issue. *Playboy* went on a worldwide search to find the most spectacular-looking woman to be the centerfold. I looked at the centerfold. She was gorgeous. Large breasts and a small, flat stomach with excellent abdominal muscles. She looked so good that I began to wonder if perhaps I could do better than my college girlfriend.

I arrive at her home in upstate New York that night. Suddenly, I lost all interest in her. This was extremely upsetting to her and me. I tried to hold the relationship together when we returned to Washington a few days later, but the feeling was gone. I broke up with her. It was like what happened to me with the girl in the summer of 1970. The closer I got to very close intimacy with a woman, the less I enjoyed it. It wasn't her fault, it was mine. I had a problem. I kept comparing these women to *Playboy* centerfolds. If they didn't fully match up, I ended the relationship. My fantasy life impaired my real life.

This pattern would repeat many times, with many different women, over the next twenty-three years (1974–97).

I graduated from George Washington University in May 1974. In August 1974 I enrolled in law school at another university named Washington: Washington University in St. Louis. I received my JD there in 1977 and then returned to my hometown of Springfield, Massachusetts.

From 1974 to 1980 I dated numerous women and had sex with four of them. All four used a female contraceptive. I did not impregnate any of them. All were single, not married. Nevertheless, I have some explaining to do. Some people, for religious or moral reasons, are opposed to premarital sex. I did not get married until 2003. I had sex with numerous women from 1974 to 2003 while unmarried. Let me tell you my personal theology on this. Feel free to skip this if you are not interested.

The Bible teaches that a man should not have sexual intercourse with a woman unless they are married to each other. The purpose of that teaching is, I believe, to prevent adultery, unwed pregnancy, and spread of sexually-transmitted disease. The Bible is not entirely clear on what is and isn't sexual "intercourse." A man's inserting his naked penis into a woman's naked vagina is "sexual intercourse." Short of that, it isn't always clear (to me, anyway) where "heavy petting" ends and "sexual intercourse" begins. Does the Bible allow an unmarried male and unmarried female to kiss and touch each other and get sexually excited? I think it does. Some people may disagree with me on that.

Beginning in 1980 or '81 and until 1996, I used a male condom every time I had sex, without exception. I believed that when a man puts a good-quality condom over his penis and inserts it into a woman's vagina, his naked penis doesn't touch her vagina. I believed that only the condom touches her vagina. Whether sex using a condom is "intercourse" and violates biblical teaching is a matter of semantics and debate. I see no reason to discuss it here. I believed it was okay for me to do. I didn't impregnate anyone. I didn't have sex with married women. These women were all single (divorced or never married) when I had sex with them. I always had the woman's consent. I had no sexual disease. My conscience was and is clear.

My goal wasn't to be sexually excited looking at all women or most women, just some women. My goal wasn't to be, or have, a particular sexual "orientation." Had you asked me my goal, I would not have said my goal is "to be straight." My goal was to find a woman I could love and marry and have a happy, monogamous sexual relationship with.

I'll tell you about a woman I had sex with in 1976. She was cute, small-breasted, and had a nice butt. I had not seen her legs because she always wore pants. We had sex. Her legs were okay but not muscular. I decided to discontinue our sexual relationship. She asked me why. I told her I prefer women more buxom. I hated myself for telling her this and she probably hated me for it too. But she asked me a question, and I answered it honestly or with a half-truth (the other half is that I like muscular women). I could not tell a lie. My guess is that many men who identify as gay have had awkward, painful (to both them and the women they reject) experiences similar to mine: telling women why these men are rejecting them.

In 1979 I began suffering headaches. I did not know why. I went to several doctors. They could not find anything wrong. I did not enjoy practicing law, so maybe it was causing me headaches. But I was sexually frustrated too. Maybe that was causing me headaches. I told a number of friends about my headaches. One friend surmised that I suffer from latent, suppressed homosexuality and the suppression is causing me headaches. I consulted a psychiatrist. I told him I like muscular women and asked him if it means I am gay. At that time, homosexuality was still unpopular.

He responded, "Don't panic. It doesn't necessarily mean you are gay." His diagnosis: mild depression.

CHAPTER 4

Soft Faces, Hard Bodies

In the 1980s, women's bodybuilding became a sport. Many women started lifting weights and building muscle. I saw it in gyms, magazines, and on TV. This was a very helpful development in my life. The type of women I like were now in style. Rather than wondering if my interest in muscular women is veiled homosexuality, I saw that many men have the same fascination with muscular women I do. I bought women's bodybuilding magazines and fantasized about the women pictured. Coincidentally, in April 1980 I briefly rekindled my relationship with my GWU girlfriend. I visited her a few times in Washington that year. I suggested she would be a great bodybuilder. She replied that she prefers dance.

Over the next five years or so, I dated four or five female bodybuilders I met at gyms and other places in my area. In 1985 I attended the most prestigious women's bodybuilding contest in the world: the Ms. Olympia at the Felt Forum (now Hulu Theater) at Madison Square Garden in New York. I paid the then-large sum of $100 to sit near the front row so I could ogle these women.

From 1986 to '88, I dated a wonderful woman much younger than I. In '86 I was thirty-three, she was nineteen. We dated steadily for two years. She had a great figure. She was fairly buxom but did not have any real muscular parts. I tried to get her into bodybuilding, and she was mildly receptive. She and I attended a women's bodybuilding contest in Worcester, Massachusetts. That was the steadiest relationship I'd had until it ended two years later. I'm not sure it was ever a really serious relationship, but we had many good times together.

While I was dating her, a woman my age who repeatedly rejected me a few years earlier suddenly became interested in me. A few years earlier, I fantasized about her. I thought that if I could have sex with any woman I know, it would be her. She had the best breasts I ever saw: big and beautiful. Nice face, nice legs. Nice person. One night in the summer of 1986 I had sex with her (this woman my age). I didn't enjoy it much. It wasn't her fault, it was mine. I learned that when a large-breasted woman lies on her back, her breasts sag somewhat to her sides. I was hoping and expecting they would be firm, upright mounds on top of her chest, but they sag to her sides. What I was hoping and expecting to be the greatest moment of my life turned out not to be. Apparently, I wanted a woman when I couldn't have her. If I eventually had her, I didn't want her. I'll always be grateful to this woman and two other large-breasted women I had sex with in the mid-1980s. They fulfilled my fantasy. My breast fixation was over. My muscle fixation was not.

One day in the late 1980s or early '90s, I was having sex with a muscular woman. She laughed and said to me, "David, you must have been gay."

I said, "What? How was I gay? You're a woman and I'm having a great time in bed with you."

She said, "I'm built like a man. You're fascinated with my muscles."

I replied, "Whatever I'm fascinated with, you're still a woman."

The relationship eventually ended, but I still smile when I think about what she said. It made me wonder: Should I be labeled by what I *think*, or by what I *do*? What I *do* is have sex with a woman. I concluded that it is better not to label at all.

Around this time (late 1980s), I was prescribed a new medication for my depression. It helped. I continue to take it today.

By the mid-1990s, there was a significant change in my sex life: I did not always feel I needed to use a contraceptive. I was in my mid-forties and meeting some women who were near fifty. They were, I think, postmenopausal. Until then, I always used, or the woman always used, a contraceptive. My sex life improved when, due to women reaching their late-forties, I did not use a contraceptive with them. I wonder how many men who have sex with men (MSM is the abbreviation used by the U.S. Centers for Disease Control) do so, not because they prefer men to women, but because no contraceptive is necessary. Of course, condoms serve a purpose in addition to contraception. They help prevent sexually transmitted diseases. But contraception itself—preventing conception of a child—is unnecessary when men have sex with men. I wonder how many women have sex with women, not because they lack interest in men but because no contraceptive is necessary. I wonder how many MSM and WSW (women who have sex with women) might develop a liking for the opposite sex when the women are postmenopausal and conception is impossible.

After numerous other brief relationships with women, I met a woman at a singles dance in early 1997. I was forty-four, she was forty-nine. We have been a monogamous couple ever since. We married in 2003. We have a great sex life together, especially for two people now sixty-seven and seventy-two. We go to the gym, lift weights, and try to stay in shape. We are very happy together.

One day in 2008, prior to the Connecticut Supreme Court's October 2008 decision holding that same-sex couples have a constitutional right to marry (*Kerrigan v. Commissioner of Public Health*), I was riding on a train from New Haven to Westport, Connecticut. I was alone. A man sat next to me. I was reading a newspaper. The paper had an article about same-sex marriage. He saw the article. I don't recall exactly who started the conversation, but he said to me, "We should be allowed to marry."

I asked who's "we."

He said, "Gay people."

I said, "I have good news for you. You can marry. You just have to marry someone of the opposite sex."

He got angry. He noticed the wedding ring on my finger. Prior to October 2008 in Connecticut, a man's wedding ring meant he's married to a woman.

He looked at the people on the train and saw six or seven other men wearing wedding rings. He said, "You guys don't know what it's like to feel excluded. You don't know what it's like to be different."

I asked what he meant by "different."

He replied, "You don't know what it's like for a man to be attracted to a man."

I said, "How do you know what I know and don't know?"

He said, "Well, I assume that you guys who are married to women are not attracted to men."

I replied, "You assume wrong. I'm sure some of these guys have been attracted to a man at one time or another. Maybe I have too." I added, "I'm not sure you and I are different at all. The only difference is, you give in to the temptation. I channel it into a heterosexual relationship."

I regard homosexual temptations the way I regard any mildly negative temptation such as overeating and other little vices. Many people have them. Some resist them. Others give in.

It reminded me of an episode from the old (1959–64) *Twilight Zone* TV series. The episode was titled "A Penny for Your Thoughts." It's a parable about temptation and the will to resist it. A bank employee, Mr. Poole, arrives at the bank in the morning. Before he enters, he purchases a newspaper. He tosses the coin onto the newsstand. The coin lands on its edge. Very rarely does a coin land this way, nearly always landing heads or tails. From the moment the coin lands on its edge, Poole can miraculously read minds. He can hear people's thoughts.

Poole enters the bank. He hears the thoughts of the bank's old, trusted bookkeeper, Mr. Smithers. Smithers is thinking about stealing money from the vault. Smithers is thinking, "At 4:30 this afternoon, I'll go into the vault like I always do. I'll take my briefcase with me, and no one will suspect a thing. I'll fill my briefcase with currency, and be on a ship to Bermuda by nightfall."

After "hearing" Smithers's thoughts, Poole sees an opportunity to be a hero. He tells the bank president what Smithers is going to do. He and the bank president go to the vault with a security guard. They want to catch Smithers as Smithers emerges from the vault with the money. Smithers emerges from the vault with his briefcase. The guard grabs it and opens it. There is no money in it. Smithers did not take any money. Smithers did his job properly—he counted the money or did whatever a bookkeeper does but did not take any money. Poole is very embarrassed. Smithers did nothing wrong. The president fires Poole and walks away. Poole then asks Smithers if Smithers was indeed thinking about stealing the money.

Smithers replies, "How did you know, Mr. Poole? It's true, of course. I was thinking of filling my briefcase with the bank's money. Yes. It's a little dream of mine. Have you ever had a dream, Mr. Poole? I have. I don't always plan on Bermuda though. Sometimes, it's Siam [now Thailand], Fiji. Beautiful, exotic places where there are no books to keep … Yes, Mr. Poole, but I'll never go through with it."

Smithers had fantasies, not plans. When it came to doing the right thing, he did the right thing. He resisted the temptation to steal. For many people, little fantasies help us get through life happier. A little imagination helps. My guess—it is just a guess—is that many (not all, but many) men with homosexual urges are capable of finding a woman to satisfy them. Some are more capable than others. I will concede, however, that a man who craves another man's penis will, or might, have difficulty finding a woman to satisfy him. But if he craves muscles rather than another man's penis, he can find a muscular woman. He may need to use his imagination a little. For me, sex is as much mental as physical. What I think, visualize, or imagine is as important as what I touch. I can't speak for other people, only myself. I am not a sex therapist. I do not give sexual advice. I am just telling you what works for me.

If I was ever tempted to have sex with a male, I resisted the temptation. Why? For the same reason I resist many temptations in life. Life is full of temptations. Every day, we face many temptations. Some we resist. Some we give in to. One of the great challenges in life is resisting negative temptations. That is why many people pray, "Lead us not unto temptation, but deliver us from evil" (Matt. 6:13). Life is full of temptations. They tempt us every day, sometimes every hour or minute. Many people pray for the strength to resist most of these temptations. Many resist homosexual temptations. Some give in.

Do I still feel homosexual temptations? I still feel many sexual temptations. Even at age sixty-seven, I feel sexual temptations every day for different types of people, just as I feel daily temptations to overeat. I'd be embarrassed to tell you all the temptations I feel. I usually resist the temptation to overeat. I always resist the temptation to touch a person in a sexual way or for sexual gratification, unless that person is my wife. What goes through my imagination is just that: my imagination.

Fittingly, the group that sang that song—"Just My Imagination"—was The Temptations. To paraphrase Freud's view of therapy with patients who have homosexual urges but want to be heterosexual, "Success means making heterosexual feelings possible, not eliminating homosexual feelings." I haven't eliminated all my sexual urges for other people, but I have achieved enough sexual gratification with my wife that my urges for other people are resistible. I resist or ignore those urges or figure out a way to satisfy those urges with my wife. Sometimes it takes a little imagination.

CHAPTER 5

My Choice

Is homosexuality a choice? Can it be "cured"? Are people "born that way"?

Homosexuality is not an "it." Homosexuality is not a "that way." Homosexuality is at least two things, maybe more: 1) urges (thoughts that go through one's head), and 2) behavior (touching someone in a sexual way). Some of these urges and actions change over time. Many people who have had homosexual sex have also had heterosexual sex. Can homosexual urges be eliminated? I don't know and don't care. Many sexual urges run through my head. I would be embarrassed to tell you some of the sexual urges I feel. I ignore or resist them, except the urges for my wife. I have not touched anyone, except her, in a sexual way since she and I became a couple in April 1997. My *mind* occasionally wanders but my *body* does not. That is my point: Everyone's mind occasionally, or even daily, or hourly, wanders into forbidden territory. The challenge is to resist the urge. The urge isn't forbidden. Giving in to the urge is forbidden. Most people face these urges every day of their lives. Think how often you wonder if you have eaten too much or drank too much. Think how often you resist the urge to overeat or overdrink.

I view homosexuality the way I view cigarette smoking. I was never a good science student, so whatever analogy I draw between cigarette smoking and homosexuality is not science. It is simply the thoughts of one man—me—who has experienced both urges. I smoked cigarettes for twenty-eight years from 1970 to '98. I think you will find the analogy interesting and perhaps informative. Read this chapter for what it's worth, which may be little or nothing. There are remarkable parallels between my history of cigarette smoking and my history of homosexual urges. Decide for yourself if anything I say here is informative.

I was born in 1953. From a very young age, I knew I wanted to smoke cigarettes when I become old enough. I enjoyed watching cigarette commercials on TV in the late 1950s and early '60s. My parents smoked cigarettes then. Nearly half of all adults smoked cigarettes then. I daydreamed about what brand of cigarettes I'd smoke when I grow up. I knew that people do not start smoking until they are at least thirteen or so. I knew that it's illegal to buy cigarettes unless one is at least eighteen or maybe even twenty-one. I knew that cigarette smoking is not good for one's health. I knew that cigarette smoking can be unsightly to people in the vicinity. Smoke gets in their eyes.

Almost all of this is true as well about homosexual sex. A boy at a very young age (younger than thirteen) might have some vague notion about what sexual behavior is and whether he prefers to have physical contact with boys or girls. At around thirteen—the age at which some boys start smoking—he may start kissing and "making out," probably with girls but possibly with boys. He is going through puberty. Like cigarette smoking, homosexual sex is unsightly to people who are opposed to it. They don't want to watch two men kiss on the lips or hold hands. Many people regard public displays of homosexual affection the way nonsmokers regard cigarette smoke. "I don't care what you do in private, but don't do it when I am sitting a few feet away," these people say. The only difference between homosexual sex and cigarette smoking in this analogy is that smoking is a health hazard while homosexual sex may or may not be a health hazard, depending on sex (male or female), sexual behavior, and medicine. In the 1980s and '90s, during the AIDS crisis, male homosexual sex was widely regarded as a health hazard. Whether it remains a health hazard today is a matter of opinion. I am not a medical doctor or other health care professional, so I will offer no opinion on it.

My parents quit smoking in 1963. Thereafter, they urged me never to smoke. So I did not smoke when I lived with them. In September 1970, I left home and traveled four hundred miles to Washington DC, enrolling at George Washington University. A few weeks into the first semester,

I began smoking cigarettes. I continued until 1998. I hid it from my parents for all twenty-eight years, although I think they suspected I smoked.

When people urged me to quit smoking, I replied, "I can't. I'm hooked. It's who I am. I'll be the last one to quit." That is what many men who have sex with men say when people urge them to quit having sex with men and, instead, try to find a woman to love.

On July 7, 1998, twenty-eight years after I began smoking, I was having difficulty breathing. I drove to the local emergency room. I told the doctor I smoke. She told me I had bronchitis. She said she expects me to recover but that the bronchitis might become chronic if I continue to smoke.

I never smoked another cigarette. Was quitting easy? No. Did I need therapy or conversion to quit smoking? No. Did my religion cause me to quit? No. I quit because I decided to quit. Did I continue to have urges? Yes. To this day, some twenty-two years after my last cigarette, I still have an occasional urge to smoke. Do I smoke? No. Why? Because it is bad for me. I'm worried I'll get hooked again. I resist the urge. Sometimes I fantasize about smoking. I tell myself, "Smoke one cigarette a day. It will satisfy the urge and not be much of a health hazard." Then I remember how I became a smoker at seventeen. In my college dorm, I had a roommate who smoked, but only one cigarette a day. He invited me to join him. I joined him. Soon for me (not him), one cigarette became five, then ten. I smoked approximately ten cigarettes (half a pack) a day from 1970 to '98. Knowing that one cigarette will lead to ten, I now resist the urge to smoke. I won't smoke even one. I have not smoked a cigarette since July 7, 1998.

Can a man who has sex with men quit having sex with men and find happiness with a woman if he wants to? My guess (again, I'm not an expert, so I am just guessing) is it depends on the man and how strongly he wants to find happiness with a woman. It depends also on the woman, or women, he meets. He needs to find one woman he can love and who will love him. It only takes one.

LGBTQ activists may argue that people who are sexually attracted to the same sex should have sex with the same sex, not the opposite sex. They argue that homosexuality and heterosexuality are equal. They argue that homosexuality is becoming as acceptable as heterosexuality. They argue that young people accept homosexuality more than older people do. They predict that in another decade or two, as the older generation dies off, homosexuality and gay marriage will be widely accepted. I am inclined to disagree. Attitudes about homosexuality may be evolving a little, but sexual anatomy is not. I expect that most people will continue to believe that the penis is designed to fit into the vagina. They will believe that that is the correct way to have sex. They will frown on other ways. They may respect the right of a person to have sex other ways, but they will frown on those ways.

The sexual urges that enter my mind are not always my choice. Who I share my penis with—a woman or man—is my choice. Does everyone have this choice? I don't know. I speak only for myself.

CHAPTER 6

Banning Conversion Therapy: Good or Bad?

The LGBTQ community conveys the impression that "conversion therapy" is a cruel effort to force gay people to be straight. The LGBTQ community often depicts "conversion therapy" as physically painful.

But the way the law defines "conversion therapy," the friendly lecture I received at age fifteen in the gym locker room in 1968 was "conversion therapy." The man or boy (I forget whether he was a teacher or student; he may have been a student teacher or assistant coach in the physical education department) who gave me that lecture noticed I had an erection when I looked at a boy. He noticed it on more than one occasion. He told me that an erect penis is designed to fit into a vagina. It was his way of telling me that girls, not boys, should sexually excite me.

If that conversation were to occur today in Connecticut, where I now live and practice law, with a fifteen-year-old boy who has homosexual urges, it might be illegal. It would depend on whether the person giving the lecture is a "health care provider." It is illegal in Connecticut for a "health care provider" to engage in "conversion therapy" with a person younger than eighteen.

Conversion therapy is defined in Connecticut General Statutes section 19a-907(1) as:

> any practice or treatment administered to a
> person under eighteen years of age that seeks to
> change the person's sexual orientation or gender
> identity, including, but not limited to, any effort
> to change gender expression or to eliminate or
> reduce sexual or romantic attraction or feelings

toward persons of the same gender. "Conversion therapy" does not include counseling intended to (A) assist a person undergoing gender transition, (B) provide acceptance, support and understanding to the person, or (C) facilitate the person's coping, social support or identity exploration and development, including, but not limited to, any therapeutic intervention that is neutral with regard to sexual orientation and seeks to prevent or address unlawful conduct or unsafe sexual practices, provided such counseling does not seek to change the person's sexual orientation or gender identity.

The therapy is illegal even if the child requests it. The statute does not define *sexual orientation*, but another Connecticut statute (section 46a-81a) defines *sexual orientation* as "having a preference for heterosexuality, homosexuality or bisexuality, having a history of such preference or being identified with such preference . . . ."

Suppose a fifteen-year-old boy (let's call him Joe) is sexually excited when he looks at his friend Bob in the gym shower. Joe talks to a Connecticut health care provider about it. "Health care provider" in Connecticut means a psychologist, medical doctor (a psychiatrist is a medical doctor), nurse, marriage and family therapist, social worker, pharmacist, hypnotist, and some other professionals. Joe tells the provider, "I get an erection when I look at Bob. Does that mean I'm gay? I don't want to be gay. I want to date girls, like Bob does." If the health care provider encourages Joe to date girls, or discourages Joe to date boys, the provider will be accused of violating the law.

What is the purpose of this law? It may have several purposes, but here is what I believe one purpose is. Many LGBTQ people want Joe to date boys. Joe is sexually excited looking at a boy, so they want Joe to behave accordingly. They want health care providers to refuse to help Joe date girls even if Joe wants to date girls and requests such help. What other possible reason can there be for a law that prohibits health care providers from helping Joe date girls? The only reason I can think of is they want him to date boys. They say Joe is gay. They might say Joe is "born that way." They want Joe to stay that way.

I'm open to discussion about this. If anyone reading this book has a better explanation for a law that prohibits health care providers from helping this boy develop a sexual interest in girls, please tell me. Why is conversion therapy illegal in Connecticut even if the boy requests such therapy and his parents agree to it?

As of February 21, 2020, approximately nineteen states and a few dozen cities or counties in the United States have banned conversion therapy on minors (younger than eighteen). That is, they ban licensed health care providers from helping a kid who has homosexual urges be heterosexual even if the kid wants to be heterosexual and requests such help. Do they ban other people (people who are not licensed health care providers) from helping the kid be heterosexual? Read the law in your state, city, or county. Decide for yourself. These laws are worded somewhat differently from state to state. Connecticut's law bans some people, but not other people, from helping the kid be heterosexual.

As I read the Connecticut law (perhaps you read it differently), it may be illegal for a Connecticut health care provider to tell Joe, a boy who has homosexual urges but wants to be heterosexual:

"The male sex organ is designed to fit into the female sex organ. That is how people reproduce. Keep that in mind. It may help you develop an interest in girls."

"The first sexual urges many kids your age experience are homosexual. Most of these kids will eventually be heterosexual. You'll see. Wait another year or two."

"It's Adam and Eve, not Adam and Steve."

"Do you want to conceive a child? If you do, marrying a man makes it very difficult. You'd have to find a woman surrogate. It is impossible to conceive a child without a woman."

"Gay and bisexual men are more likely to develop HIV than heterosexual men are."

Each of those statements may be construed as a "practice or treatment administered to a person under eighteen years of age that seeks to change the person's sexual orientation," according to Conn. General Statutes section 19a-907(1). Each statement seeks to change Joe from homosexual orientation to heterosexual. It encourages Joe to date girls, not boys.

The provider may argue that the statement about HIV is true. According to a September 2019 document "HIV and Gay and Bisexual Men"[6] on the U.S. Centers for Disease Control (CDC) website, of the 38,739 new HIV diagnoses in the United States (the fifty states, District of Columbia, American Samoa, Guam, Northern Mariana Islands, Puerto Rico, Republic of Palau, and US Virgin Islands) in 2017, 27,000 (70 percent) were among adult and adolescent gay and bisexual men. The provider may argue that the statement "seeks to prevent or address unlawful conduct or unsafe sexual practices,"[7] but the LGBTQ community and Connecticut regulators may argue that the statement is not "neutral" with regard to sexual orientation and does seek to change the boy's sexual orientation. They'll argue that the statement violates the law.

---

[6] https://www.cdc.gov/hiv/pdf/group/msm/cdc-hiv-msm.pdf (last visited Feb. 21, 2020).

[7] Conn. Gen. Stat. § 19a-907(1).

Suppose a school nurse teaches sex education in Connecticut. A boy in her class is attracted to boys. If she teaches that an erect penis is designed to be inserted into a vagina, she may violate the law. Her teaching will be construed as an effort to change the boy's sexual orientation from homosexual to heterosexual. To comply with the law, she may have to give equal time to discussing homosexual sex. She may have to teach that the penis can be inserted into a mouth, anus, and hand as well as a vagina. Banning conversion therapy arguably violates her freedom of speech and religion. Courts will have to decide.

It seems to me (this is just my view; you may have a different view) that the true goal of banning conversion therapy is not to "protect" kids but to cause kids who think they might be gay to decide they are in fact gay. Its goal is to change Q kids (the Q in LGBTQ can mean "questioning") to G (gay), L (lesbian), or B (bisexual). Its goal is to funnel sexually confused kids into the LGBTQ camp rather than the "straight" camp. It allows gay-affirming statements. It allows the therapist to tell Joe, the fifteen-year-old boy who is sexually excited looking at Bob: "It's okay to be attracted to

Bob. It's okay to be gay. It's okay for you to ask Bob for a date. Maybe Bob feels the same way about you." Any statement that might cause or encourage Joe to date girls is legally risky. This is why some people refer to the "ban conversion therapy" movement as the "stay gay" movement. It is, or seems, designed to persuade people with homosexual urges to stay gay and not convert to straight.

I agree that conversion therapy should not be *forced* on Joe. It should be available only if Joe requests it. If his parents request it for him, I am inclined to think the therapist should ask Joe if Joe also requests it, and provide therapy only if Joe answers yes.

I have no opinion about therapies that are physical or invasive. I know very little about them. I have read about them but have no idea if they actually are happening these days or happened much in the past. Banning some types of conversion therapies on minors may be good. Banning all types of conversion therapies on minors is bad, in my opinion.

I don't like the term "conversion therapy." It is a misnomer. That is why I usually (not always) put quotation marks around it. In my view, a fifteen-year-old boy who has homosexual urges but wants to be heterosexual is not trying to "convert." He has a penis. He has learned or decided that a penis is designed to eventually, when he is an adult, fit into a vagina. He is trying to do what he is designed to do. Helping him date girls is not "therapy." *Therapy*, according to a leading dictionary, is a "remedial treatment of mental or bodily disorder." I'm inclined to think the boy doesn't have a disorder. He just wants to do what he is anatomically designed to do. His homosexual urges may be a bit of an obstacle but are not a disorder. Since they are not a disorder, "therapy" is the wrong word. Efforts to help him be heterosexual are efforts to help him be what he wants to be.

Nevertheless, some states, cities, and organizations call those efforts "conversion therapy." This raises a question: Isn't all therapy "conversion therapy"? Isn't all therapy designed to "convert" someone one way or another? Why not call weight-loss therapy or alcohol rehabilitation therapy "conversion therapy"? If you help someone convert from 300 pounds to 200 pounds, or from drinking whiskey to drinking water, why not call it "conversion therapy"? How the term "conversion therapy" came to refer only to sexual orientation "conversion therapy" puzzles me.

If a boy has homosexual urges but wishes to eventually, when he is old enough, marry a woman, I think it should be legal, not illegal, for a health care provider to help him be heterosexual. Banning conversion therapy makes it illegal.

Some people say conversion therapy is an effort to make gay kids straight. *Forced* conversion therapy is an effort to make gay kids straight. Conversion therapy that a kid *requests* is an effort to help the kid be what the kid wants to be.

What they call "conversion therapy" is often a simple anatomy lesson. The simple anatomy lesson teaches that the penis, when erect, is designed to fit into a vagina. If you look at where the penis and vagina are on the male and female bodies, and think about how people reproduce, it appears that the penis, when erect, is designed to fit into a vagina. The LGBTQ community doesn't like that lesson. They want to ban as many people as they can from giving and hearing that lesson. They have difficulty banning a father from giving his son, or clergyman giving a parishioner, that lesson. The First

Amendment to the U.S. Constitution gets in the way. But they can, or think they can, ban licensed health care providers from giving children that lesson. For a violation, the state can revoke the provider's license. Some health care providers are challenging those bans on First Amendment grounds. If a boy has an urge to kiss boys, the LGBTQ community doesn't want people to talk him out of it. They probably cannot prevent the boy's parents and clergy from talking him out of it but they can, or think they can, prevent licensed health care providers from talking him out of it.

Banning conversion therapy, it seems to me, is like banning weight-loss therapy. Is being overweight an illness? Often not. Yet even if it's not an illness, many overweight people want to lose weight. Many seek therapy to help them lose weight. Does this therapy shame them about being overweight? Sometimes it might. Are overweight people "born that way"? Do they have a "fat gene"? Many overweight people think so. "I didn't choose to be overweight," many overweight people say. Even if homosexuality is not an illness, many people who have homosexual urges don't want to be homosexual. Many wish to be heterosexual. "Conversion therapy" is not necessarily based on the notion that homosexuality is an illness. It is based on the fact that many people who have homosexual urges want to be heterosexual. It aims to give them what they want. Can overweight people eat less and feel satisfied? Some can. Can people with homosexual urges have heterosexual sex and feel satisfied? Some can.

People who want to ban conversion therapy say conversion therapy doesn't work. Does weight-loss therapy work? It works on some people, not others. I am guessing that conversion therapy works on some people, not others. It depends, I am guessing, on how skilled the therapist is, how motivated the patient is, and if the patient meets a suitable person of the opposite sex.

The New York State Office of Mental Health reported in 2016 that only half of the teenage population identifies as "exclusively heterosexual."[8] The other half is attracted to the same sex occasionally or often. I am guessing it was always that way. I am guessing that since the beginning of time, half

---

[8] "Meeting the Mental Health Needs of LGBTQ New Yorkers," June 2016, https://omh.ny.gov/omhweb/resources/newsltr/2016/june-2016.pdf (last visited Feb. 21, 2020).

of all teenage boys were sexually attracted to a boy at one time or another. I was. I am guessing that most of them, as men, had sex only with females. The Gallup organization in 2017 estimated that only 4.5 percent of the U.S. population is LGBT.[9] The large gap between the percentage of boys who have homosexual urges (50 percent) and the percentage of men who have sex with men (4.5 percent or fewer) upsets the LGBT community. If a boy has homosexual urges, they want him to date boys, not girls. When he reaches adulthood, they want him to date men. If he marries, they want him to marry a man. They often claim that 10 percent, not 4.5 percent, of the population is gay. In 2019, GLAAD (formerly known as Gay & Lesbian Alliance Against Defamation) called on the TV industry to "make sure that 20 percent of series regular characters on primetime scripted broadcast series are LGBTQ by 2025."[10]

---

[9] Justin McCarthy, "Americans Still Greatly Overestimate U.S. Gay Population," https://news.gallup.com/poll/259571/americans-greatly-overestimate-gay-population.aspx (last visited Feb. 21, 2020).

[10] "Where We Are on TV 2019-2020," p. 4, https://www.glaad.org/sites/default/files/GLAAD%20WHERE%20WE%20ARE%20ON%20TV%202019%202020.pdf (last visited Feb. 21, 2020).

If a fifteen-year-old boy today gets an erection watching boys in the locker room, as I did at fifteen, the gay-straight alliance or LGBTQ club at his school (they didn't have such clubs in 1968 when I was fifteen) might encourage him to "come out." They might encourage him to tell the whole school he is gay and thereby label himself in a way that will be difficult to un-label (everyone will remind him that he "came out") if, a year later, he decides, as I did at sixteen, to date girls. They might discourage him, at fifteen while he feels gay, from seeking or receiving any type of professional counseling to help him date girls. Many of them don't want him to date girls. They want him to date boys. That, I believe, is the true motivation, or one motivating factor, behind laws banning conversion therapy.

That is one reason I wrote this book: to expose the whole truth about laws banning conversion therapy.

Another reason I wrote this book is I wondered what I would do if I were fifteen today (2020) in Connecticut and sexually excited looking at a boy. Some people would tell me I am gay. Some people would tell me I have no choice about it. Some people would tell me that my only choice, if I want to be happy, is to date boys.

I think I'd want more choices than that. I'd want the option—not the requirement, but the option—to date girls, like most other boys do. I would want the option to eventually marry a woman. I wouldn't want to be told I can't. I'd seek help and information. I would find little help or information on the internet. I would talk to a school psychologist. The psychologist would probably refuse to help me date girls. Connecticut law prohibits conversion therapy on minors.

I could go to a priest, minister, or rabbi who is not a licensed health care provider, but the clergy are somewhat divided on the topic. A few years ago, a Jewish man told me he teaches sex education at a Conservative synagogue. There are basically three types of synagogues: Orthodox, Conservative, and Reform. I knew that Reform Judaism accepts gay marriage. I thought Conservative Judaism does not. I asked this man, "What do you tell them about gay marriage?"

He replied, "I tell them it's kosher," meaning acceptable.

So, if I were fifteen today, I'd be frustrated. I'd find few, if any, resources to help me achieve my goal: eventually marrying a woman and being happy with her. Of course, I don't know for certain if that would be my goal if I were fifteen today. I'm sixty-seven today. Society's acceptance of homosexuality and gay marriage is somewhat greater today than it was when I was fifteen. But if I were fifteen and my goal were to be like most other boys—heterosexual—I'd want to explore whether I can achieve that goal. I'd want to explore whether I have the potential to be happily heterosexual. I would find few resources to help me.

So, I wrote this book. It is one man's (my) true story. If it helps anyone, I am pleased.

ABOUT THE AUTHOR

David A. Robinson lives in Connecticut with his wife. He earned his BA from George Washington University in 1974 and JD from Washington University in St. Louis in 1977. He practiced law in Massachusetts from 1977 to 2008 and now practices in Connecticut.